Cover image   "Melissa and Jim"
by   Samuel Morgan

Author photo by   Ben Ruggiero

Published in the United States by   Fence Books
                                New Library 320
                                University at Albany
                                1400 Washington Avenue
                                Albany, NY 12222
                                www.fenceportal.org

Book design by   Rebecca Wolff

Fence Books are distributed by   University Press of New
England

                                www.upne.com

and printed in Canada by   Westcan Printing Group
                                www.westcanpg.com

Library of Congress Cataloguing in Publication Data
        Huffman, Jibade-Khalil [1981–]
          19 Names for Our Band/ Jibade-Khalil Huffman

Library of Congress Control Number: 2008920759

ISBN 1-934200-10-7
ISBN 13: 978-1-934200-10-0

first edition

Fence Books are published in partnership with the University at Albany and the New York State Writers Institute, and with help from the New York State Council on the Arts and the National Endowment for the Arts

19 names for
our band

jibade-khalil huffman

fence books
albany, new york

19 names for
our band

jibade-khalil huffman

contents

i.

ii.

iii.

iv.

notes
acknowledgements

i.

prayer

We were werewolves before we started fighting crime. Before we would gather in a bar and grill near the high school. Once it was dark

once every yard has the same commitment they all seem alike. I'm terrified of big bridges and you are afraid of getting hit by a car. I have been to the hospital twice this year because there is music

because I'm in love with an uptown girl doesn't mean I was struck by lightning for ten seconds last night; as confused as I was I forgot to include misfortune; your disappearance from horizon   .

from anyone seeing.

very early in the life of jerome (i)

My mother begins by letting on that she is missing, my mother admits I never had the "terrible twos" and I was sent to a military academy of my own volition. I told her she needn't help me pack, I would not forget my underwear and a field guide and I let her sharpen the razor blade and I let her tighten my bolo tie into a knot I could not remember. My earliest memory is of my mother asking if I had *the dummies* or she asked her sister on the phone, "do you know my husband's one true love?" She was given the paperback edition of "School Children Led Into A Basement" for their anniversary from my father with a card that read "this was not on sale." This year I will enter a beauty pageant and start courting a boy who calls me his little big mouth bass and I have many loafers, a pair for every occasion.

19 names for our band

1. Handjob
2. Summercamp
3. Pastor for the racing boat, pow-wow
4. Bonfire and Jamboree.
5. Seventeen cars piled up.
6. Underwater is
7. An invitation to compare the incomparable tone of a Kohler and Campbell with any other piano.
8. Adult dog is the new unicorn.
9. Took is a Canadian syllable.
10. Jimmy Riffle, I told you so.
11. Tennis skirt for tennis elbow.
12. For one night and one night only
13. Apache Ramos leading the airlift
14. of all boys who have forsaken me
15. Mitch Rider and the Three Ring Binder
16. the pace at which describing water
17. became a psychic joke
18. where they know your end
19. and bribed will never say them.

framework

This is called angled feet this is called
separate parts of faces
this is about body parts it's called
wide-eyed radio hour

this is called exits and
this titled "these roads have low shoulders

those roads that are shared roads
with horses," the story is about

character archetypes and if
the will became profane for

subtracting curves from planes from
clamor subsisting on "she had

her gun all ready"
it was about snow perfume
it had as title
the arc of the narrative

the materiality of the sonata
hinges on the figure
yielding to the spontaneous
break of a rib.

Tract house poems are
not about suburbia they are not titled thrush

they are framed by subject
as outline for
specific plant growth
certain color and
scope, shape of dress

concentricity and
enjambed
general assembly of
staves rocking into ropes "with certain

persons hanging."

"When delivering make-up..."

When delivering make-up
for the neighborhood watch association's
second annual fundraiser
for our statues restoration
I imagine I am the guidance counselor
on television's Degrassi High. Every
colored one naming Jamal
in the advice I've given
instrumental to the parent's
own wish of first a doctor
then nearly as well
to leave the house
just because

your family has seen you naked once
does not mean they want to see
you naked again on the occasion
of Dr. King's birth
which was this year the day
we handed over the packages.
My life's work concerns revealing
celebrities enabled
secret lines of the guides demise
to truth telling of the last
and last letter
in which Star Jones talks about
her man her
wedding the rumors
and the lies.

very early in the life of jerome (ii)

Besides the song "Listen For the Hollows in the Surface of the Ocean" only you can hold me back from the ledge. What began with us burying objects, ends in building a fence to mark in case we forget them. I've told you so and I've told you so and I've told you so you'll defend me. At the trial they've exhibited the plates of the savages, which are their gloves; and their hats are their cups and the skirts are their saucers.

diamond zones

Rehabilitation of
the burned parent

in a rowboat
a knock-kneed

the mind tries
to find speaking

Dutch chime
picture plane, sometimes
the child tears
at my mouth

so it seems
he can collide

free of envy
into rocks

after the
dinner mint

plate cleared away, while
others still in need of
obedience, seeming
in thumbs trapped
under fallen
of flake of ledge.
For the sake of

good planning
I have never once traced
the bullet to its beginning
as a stopper in a jar. That

which he will remember
as true, agreeing with me, that
ordinary listing. Eastern
hog's call; Cezannes' "diamond zones"
hour of burning hooks
caught broke in space

the third try
in as many years
on my life, all
the same night

these and those
like them, said to
have been held captive.

very early in the life of jerome (iii)

We found fifty dollars in a box in the shed back of your
uncle's. Sometimes during rush hour traffic we stand on opposite
sides of the street and debate taking the money, that man, he can
read your lips and this is the only way he won't hear us. As for
insisting that I've never looked better than when I had a cold and it
appeared I was crying, I will say that you never looked better than
when you told me you didn't live here and that man pointing the
gun at me wasn't one of your relatives.

abigail

1.
An abigail, improbable line
cut of the forest, from aboveboard
for five dollars the ears of corn

were shucked and turned over
the surface. The die or dice used.
The tycoon armed himself
with a racket edge. What stage

as that, as ours, in romance taken on
in absence, the color saffron; delirious.
A hurdler clearing a hurdle
in the low hurdles; our months are
out of sorts, rails immediate
angels-on-horseback. The colonel

has commanded that the acres
appear less wandering
than they are. An angora, sack's cloth

2.
the figures in the painted hunting
crowded in the gesture, Romagnola
the husk of hares the murmuration

of starlings the siege
of bitterns the Giant Panda is
a different matter. In its case it is

very hard to believe that it
is a member, the largest
of the raccoon family and not
the bear it so resembles.

for all that is well with the novel

The good doctor, right reverend Mr.

panting effect now in Beaumont
Jackson having his daughter
to the lake too late

as in Niagara; the benefit
of taking to the streets
to align the objects in a swell: how

fitting it is to begin the landscape

at its center; sky and common parcels
can align themselves, if in the foreground
there is a figure momentarily

he must have his back turned
in the detail he has found labels
to inspect in rummaging before: of

the magazine we are to believe this

how he posed with the basket and
the box, the accompanying story has
the actors own captions

speaking the voice of the general
the least
of his roles

phoned in
to great acclaim.

auburn system

          The auburn
system of the loop

the trophy
is of an outboard motor.
We have held

the wheels

of the wagon and vowed
they be pushed

into a pattern, timing
of chairs. Forty five

piano tunings, the disguise

of the shed

the night
attending

the applause the

          rowers all watching

from the Isleboro Ferryslip

the seams that have glorified
the body, threaded

close to ground.
       What good
the buried do, still

under the memorial
hairbrushed, bundles
wound out from spools

mended

into attention.

like molly in *the mountain lion*

Stately, thinking they are pills, runaway carriages
that upset their drivers into patches of thorns and boarded up
into disguise, introduces his chapter to Whilomville Stories by quoting
from a letter Beer attributes to Crane:
'If the Whilomville Stories seem like Little Lord Fauntleroy to you you
are demented and I know   that you are

joking besides," a bastard consciousness or something even more
complicated a time
when interested in
adventure.
Crude and eager too are the young Afrikaner men who surround. Great
laughers and jokers and pinchers of bottoms and
players of pranks. Inasmuch as we are interested in the more common
practice of blasphemy and. Certainly, that is what we want; we want
in general that

that is to be rebelled against; admitted mass of direct address about
theology and ritual heretofore than I
than I, on the way to mass.
Jean said that,
looking for an antidote to her mother's Scotch

Presbyterianism, the typing chore Jean seemed to accept as a daughterly
duty, that when
she tried to shout her down and said, "Really, he found it easy," she said
"how long is the world a wedding arranged languorously," pointed

to Helen and Jean and it is how many times since we have taken the
opposite side on bald exhaustion? Off away on one then another, until
one morning forced

into nationwide emphasis on slump of sweater shoulder part disrupted
new and ominous
social actor, Bazarov, the Nihilist.

sonnet

So long does reason go
dispelling shine, eggs to locate

beneath the plants
of the ravine. You will not make

a toll booth our only excursion
at the border as well

there are Cyclops and parades
best viewed from seventh grade—

in some form or other where
are the child stars
of yesteryear, gun runner

when you need him, grace
turning heavy
honey into glue.

notes on camp

You have wanted only
a kind of sibling
to go along
with other activity, limbs
in perilous end
what happened
to milling around

and begging forgiveness.
The rain as a distraction
but for the hard of hearing

you can say
what you want
about his hairstyle

and take for granted
they can see
what you are wearing.

the blowjob pictures

If that's what you look like
when you cum
I have exaggerated
the effort involved

modeling clothes
at the broadcast
of the surface of the moon
your mother as I remember
in the drive-in
with her eyes bugged out
at the reunion
there is no way to leave

their subdivision
except following
the truck towing our car

when we get out of this
I will die at the last part
in the street, or

in bed with the radio
for some reason, dialing the radio
in the middle of the film

they all strip down
to their underwear
in the nightclub, going bazookas

in a scrimmage with
the doorman and the owner
In the parking lot
at a reading of
the castration notice, when
I am backstage where
everyone is getting blowjobs and
everyone else is taking pictures.

wilderness literature

What intimate, white center

of competing flames, starling
who was afraid that day

for what life, what has only

meant a drum contained
whole order described in titles

third in order, as was tardy again

when in, without ending.
As to the gas-fire, with the ash rock

with the simple vow

for the meantime, at last sight that
sallow pool whose hedge ending

what bride arrives through
terrible hills in "wilderness literature"
if suddenly by type made high

on hers, a fortieth, every leaning

of any breath than needed
distance of four dances

ocean scattering Hank

blood of the killer, Madison
on struck at the throat

very early in line

for the room
after the text, "Mermaid

and the Minotaur" foretaste

of bride's saying
"Mystery In The Lane," "Save One
For The Other." Nonesuch

neck as hers
as the academy

invisible ink; invisible Black Alaska

poles at heat and different speed.

very early in the life of jerome (iv)

There were ashes on the lips of their glasses and pins in
their hair a way I imagined was dangerous. I met my first wife on
one of these occasions, trying with a quarter and a promise she
would buy me a drink after we finished dancing. The minute you
get back they'll be playing our song again. I will leave you before
you have to exaggerate the features of your apartment, promise me
breakfast. At least pin me down on the windshield and lead me to
tears, showing the signs and the side effects, the attendant worry
of finishing the phrase: much as these men and this clerk from
the grocery, four years ago and I couldn't sleep so I knew and so.
Of course all my life I've wanted to run for senator in this state, if
not here, then in Michigan, with the answer I gave that assured
everyone I was ready.

poem

When I am older
I know I will

be sure of
phantom pain approaching
the island. In a lurid turn

in a parenthetical
apparatus

under duress
without any
the regular charm. For fifty years

important, good parts
of an hour with

the technology
of girl infatuated

who go salvaging cans
for a hammer to smash

who were always doing
Magic Johnson and have
an itch about the crotch
entirely toned down
in the feature film.

to nabokov

Our worst fears have come true
and are obedient
starting fires

at the wave pool the only
capable defender of lust
had let the light off

and come running to see
what we were up to

above a symbol of the first
several languages explained
in respective replicas
"with the lectern
at which he wrote:"

where in cold and cranes
what rose appears
Dear,

       Greatest pleasure
       as overgrown
       by pairs of pants.

sonnet

In this country you have
never named your child
"rattle," "that's

for saints and I
am a man she held." "A stopwatch"
one such haberdasher

his saying "theatrical figures, three colored—

in dining cars."

The illustration
of its walls; why it is
the variety of the ax in hand, guiding

a tarp over her, the
French school of doting
Founders Day, each former name.

a maritime

The nearness of the body to, perhaps
an able seaman, in order to end in palm
to leave by eight and that

that has the admiral charging
into relapse
his cat by his lap
before he was rescinded

by the Marshal of the Royal Air Force
describing an advance of storms
from the shelter of his chair
in back of the ballroom
as both the cunning and all
about him blue.

Who was disturbed for the following months
in no particular order in the early 80's by the
bill gone unpaid for the device which heals
all arms and made it so
one could put on a bracelet
without aid of other persons. In May
then in April

the leading aircraftsman
in a series of streets guarded by aircraftsmen
who had to rise for the post
at an hour earlier than usual
and had
to stop
reading the biography

of Louisa May Alcott at eleven thirty
in the night previous, said to
the marshall

"My bed
is a motion of sores
left by others

while you have
only to consider the effect
of debts concentration
upon debt."

A quartermistress may display tea
on her table and be also
sickened by the matter
she may think it only
our lives as they are slowed

or the sun when it is setting
the feminine rhyme; other nature
that does not corrupt and ends
in dim as bland as that
is after. It goes

"that when she had the lance-jack over
for laughs and for a bath
near the wherry before ten
minutes before they passed
in a hurry, to that

the rehearsal of dances, the toe-dance
and can can that
ends by walking.

"And what is more, but the glare of dust..."

And what is more, but the glare of dust
of periods, in occurrences. Are the waves of smoke
that hover above merely the remnants of a teething?
Crumpled holler? Still if there is

a chance for Galax, Virginia. The Hotel Fontainebleau
what will peeled paint say for itself?
its mother boxing its ears
Where went the houses and billboards?

Pillars like workers hands
Away from the beaches, nineteen-fifty two or earlier
my father had but the limbs that kept us all
from crumbling

nineteen-fifty three or earlier, for a dollar and a car
and a boy, for the attention accorded
a manuscript for advertisements. I
in the foreground. You in a chair

saying to friends with your back turned
to the cusp of your hair
that there are more drop out children to be had
in dangerous weapons and jitterbugs. The

next to one another, last two
stations from the train. Jacob
Lawrence, wearing a sailor suit, there's no way
like the more that often celebrated way.

Wants to look at me and laugh.
had taken you out
on a street line. Nineteen
fifty-four or sooner. Number 10

in a series of afternoon trips to look at seals
for all your forcing of moods, standing in souplines
here is an afternoon trip to see a gambler put into the street—
those crags in his face.

Chesterfield
Dallas, Texas—with a boring postcard in his hand, pointing
at you, to draw
with an old camera
blank expressions. The privilege of sitting next to one another.

for indian hidden

In Los Angeles
we watched   Lord of the Rings
for the first time

before I
would usually
just zone out
and eat cereal

gathering the phone
to mouth

watchwords
dependence on warmth
really

I wanted a daybed
whole pound
to dictate

lyrics for
flannelette shirt and Higginbotham

to Mrs. Taylor's house   for Indian hidden

substitute
on the ride home
ceiling fan

glad to have made
your acquaintance
the heart is
a toxic shape
for civilized meeting

why I was leading
"the children's game"   in front of

dovecote
honor
is their name   and Tippi
is their name
like

blanket spanks a bottom
sometimes the card reads
four of five ways
to train the paper   explanation

of uncle paced
at long distance

in the month since
uniform   juvenilia   marmalade
alarm for

two tables
four sets of chairs   and

rest period as   famed for
one hundred dollars.

on television

There are never enough plates
to go around; some evenings our cousins
have to eat out of their hands their
mother at least has saucers arranged
in front of her; their father spilled his tea
for lack of something to catch on
when.

        He got up from the table, groping
the first thing to hold on to. In real life
fluttering hands mean only fluttering hands
for instance, his kicking has little to do
with the life of his mother. On television
that garment
is white that kept her warm
on the balcony; you cannot see
for instance, any
of any crumbs
stitched in its body
gathered in its face.

if we believe theory

we have been in
"a lavish household"

how different I am

from your body
holding myself

if I were

pressed up against you
we would understand

"the more general motion."
Unbearable

retention rate and rate
of tardy making

all of us tardy
mirrored by

the ensuing book report

on "the nudity"
as a means of

"the example;"
on a platform.

Behind nations
there are classes

adrift in

a great terror
showing the trapdoor

where I
just wanted to demonstrate

some part
I claimed to know.

very early in the life of jerome (v)

I have been trying to see his privates, trying to see his privates and he says I should take his clothes off first. Then he has to make himself available in the pantry and in the living room in case someone comes asking. He has to turn me over and introduce me to the floor. The floor is sometimes carpeted and sometimes his brother James commands his dogs to tear out the carpet and bring it to him at home. Then this is replaced and James uses those swaths not everywhere destroyed to sniff, to get the dogs to go back and sometimes they attack the wrong place and take the shoelaces of the faculty of the middle school.

where are the negroes in hartford, connecticut?

When we wake up
there is a banner
for the National
Rifle Association hanging
in our backyard
the children are gathered

and our neighbor
apologizes for late
beginning his remarks:
where are the negroes
in Hartford, Connecticut, where
is a crossing guard
when you are required
to hear the instruction:
if you are ready
you should clap
if you are standing
you should sit down
attached to an object
under anesthesia
with
the memorabilia
as a prize for
who can fastest
induce sleep
where they are there
to show
what is and

what is
not missing.

funeral, mineral, vegetable

In a responsible fashioning
of bows onto illness

make sure your face
is not recognizable
and be there by four o'clock
quoting entirely
the paragraph
by heart I do not mean
all things had better fit
in a packet
invented for subduing
the equator. The effort

of a million letters and calls
to restore a border
between houses

and the sea
is under martial law
and if you think about it
they are offering the same brand
of the same model
at a better price
in the trunk of their car
past the shore
there are poisonous snakes
at the bottom.

very early in the life of jerome (vi)

Regarding mischief, of an orphanage vanished from dry land, one can say he hates the placement of dirt on top of the city, but that he loves the dirty men who are its inhabitants. That stand the oxen to be slaughtered—these are the suspects I wish to visit. His impulse in giving elaborate directions to the home, the story of how one car was stranded in a driveway for which it was not intended, all the parties involved having complicated family arrangements, the one exception is a great-granddaughter of the original misses. She was told she had thirty days to evacuate or else to find a husband and show all the signs of being pregnant. There is little chance of our remaining calm while fielding questions, while becoming rich, while convention tells us where we should bury them.

translations of your heart's desire

The waves pull
the wall from
the wallpaper

the drugstore
was out of Pampers
but they have

sometimes parted
their wings

and sprouted lips
and are padlocking
their arms to the ice
to frighten tourists
so you can
go fuck yourself.

"Anyone can purchase flags..."

Anyone can purchase flags
and everyone can exclaim
dynamite from a balcony
it never troubles me none
here to have emptied

pearl from on a strand, here
a harbinger, there a conks-fire
dear,

my hair alight substance
separated on the
eighth note in eight days divided
by fire from the killer
whose ill cannot come if
through a door, tongue estranged

if on good terms
with an invention
preventing sleep, with the
officer in guest appearance

in end of this season
of misplacing patrol cars
and badge and baton so
no one believes him.

poem beginning with a line by edward mckeever

          "Dan Eldon's sister Amy
more rockabilly singers,"
Ralph Reed and
Georgia forwarding
the troops to

keep the blacks
latter day consequence
of dilemma

of the old guard.
Awful wedlock
of the "goodness
in your heart"
ne'er do well
of the stations
of the cross
your friend, Harris Feinsod.

why on what way/nat turner b-side

Same story of
being jostled on a bus.

To any who

think of such elucidation
of the phrase
of
before where
so much of corners
anywhere

there's colored lights

Washington
delirium

as
and does the same sometimes
the heights all
spark unerring

cause enough
1956 a
thicket
a
rushing sound
if with them around
and branches

the wisps at last
that live

on a bending ground
and is the next with them to go

in a string drawn out along each other
they say
they've had enough.
Say it's butchered
laugh, stagger, plumbed
space
as

after Syracuse
Barstow.
Course faced
Nat Turner riding down the mountain
fire crackling around him.
If this time even

with my elbow up your skirt
as scheduled as
same time signature.
Bold and

counted over
the week

plaited traits
we cannot pretend
I have found

the cherry thin of shoulder slope
lists for certain
believable terms
you're

set up beside your door screen you're
telling us

in a low-going evening

"all shall be well known." You've

set down the spill
for the sink
on the door handle. You're

furnishing songs and

you are furnishing rooms
with singing

and you've
furnished songs
before.

in an uncurling game

I spy
you have
the sheets in your hand

the outside-of-night-light
with the flecked curtain
balled into your hand.

I have to keep
telling myself
in varied tones
several times
slumped over myself
my arms around my knees

in a large chair
with the lamp out

only the blue from
the gas from
the stove

that

the glass
grudged around my ankles
is a racing edge

that it is

in the light of table lamps
where the grass slips low
as slow as paper.

I see
in a small skip of winter and
I say where before a turn—
as I have
separated the colors
from the other colors

all of what was
scissored up with my hairs from out of the tub
goes heavy

its where

I see you are seeing
housetops recede into newsprint

and if it is

what follows
in the story
that you are asking
then I
will give you

a whole phrase-of-lines about
the gray of bruises

with ringing sounds, with

sleight-of-hand figments.

I say

we draw out on the carpet a map to show
all the faces are strange. I say

lets give away the trick to rooms

and I

can see

you have gone on ahead
to the windowsill and
in a plainsong
you are saying
the words
to an old cheer.

I know
how this
is going to end.

I spy
it has the sense of glowed lights
coming through the water washing
up on stairs from before.

Its with organ and piano songs

it's with pointed and
circle flags hung from the roof.

four inter-titles for our music video

One governs oneself
in disputable terms, how

willing a witness is
to declare others harmed
when it is he who grieves
with

any of steam left of
the kettle and glow below
stoves furthest eye
covered or not with apron

having it out as though
he were never
bewildered by light.

"Those turned quiet by knives, by night..."

Those turned quiet by knives, by night
in shrill, the possibility
of children stove off from sleep
held in her arms. This was so

the blinds might not arrive, carried
in wind from once set in a window
twice to pry
some space from her lap, occupied or not

by one child, had second
gone pacing; those that held
several brands. Colored and shaken
effect of a rocking horse and

trembling, to mark on walls to
leave on names

on a landable room
that hawk attacks.

guaranteed swahili

It was in sleet that he arrived
by another misreading

he was an hour late
for the sentence, "counter

smothered in feathers"; in others
like it no mention of place

was made. The effect only
of girl on seams, in

her own jeans
into margins of the earth

trespassed, into the margins
of the earth—in villanelles

the victim is given
an hour from the town

to complain its distance
upon resorting to the tape

in guaranteed Swahili
his passing unannounced.

juliet of the spirits

Theory of sea serpents, mascot
bringer of luck, in hunting superstitions
rate of the blank face regarding
spread of noxious gases

chained to the dulcet that the
age of a rattlesnake
can be told
by its rattles, cursed among

fox superstitions, triplet of
imperfect bound, definition
for resurrected plain.
Every line

of John's agenda that the heart
is on the left side. Seventh
and ninth month
baby superstitions. Rice thrown
at weddings, world in which

confession naming bluff. School on
the second floor; four superstitions
that snakes
will not crawl over a hair rope
bulls do not see red, rabbit
and wolverine superstitions.
We cross ourselves

for various reasons, jinx accidentally
a string as cure or aid to memory
camphor superstitions, woolen
sock around the neck the most

harmless form of scarf tied
in an anchor hitch
place folding
into your hands
and left with other ruins.

"Oftener, golden rule; nude..."

Oftener, golden rule; nude.
Now blurry from
the salt-shook; at the meeting
of the camera club
Sadie shown into open
thrown from her seat
as the

train came. Her purse spurned

full of tablets
to cure

a weakling child.
In that line

the questioning of measures
now that
they have often switchblades

and are distinguished

by bandanas; that night

after the shopping center
in the parking lot there
were seventeen of them sitting
cross-

legged in a circle; now they follow
her inside the building
and separate into pairs; now there

are two days later

agents everywhere
in a disguise; fuses lined
up, eroding

in self defense, now boarding
on the last track.

"You would suppose that. In solving the way..."

You would suppose that. In
solving the way.
Out of the window. That
you have solved the bundling of the
parachute up under yourself. And out of
the window. Going into the neighbors.
In their yards on top of them you would
suppose that you could ask—wherein
falling, would straddle the grass. At the
motion, in lifting full sides of walls right
out of the way; in dusting some of the
debris off of your slacks—and should
like to ask what of tall hills that are tall
hills and air skydiving that was itself. In
solving the way out of the window that
you have solved the bundling up of the
crash on the lawn that was itself.
By meaning other people—tall
hills that are tall hills—there you are in
a row, atop the grass, beside yourself.
With occasion for especially other
bodies racked with the wet untied atop
the lawn. You should say figured colors
coming down, you should say blue
light coming down for a whole month;
flowers trundled, all there, by all the
many others, makers and winners,
grasping at flowers to hand them in
baskets. Drivers down winding roads,
down tall hills to rush in and parachute
all about atop the lawn.

palimpsest

The chartreuse, in an album
called, "The Crude Jokes"
the bric-a-brac, glow particular

without hearing
the one violet, its lake of many
black bonnets

aiming the starlet
beginning with whir
at a time the

body is gone
and teary
heart of the hammock

boy's prize of
a gumball bank
swung in a circle

even forty dollars
under Jesus Rock.
Palimpsest, had written

600 for 600 tiles.
By diapers white
to see a shadow.

On worm silk as particular
unburied tine
of phobia, number five

to a direction
for our vacuum for
rounding linens around

the former, boxed
parts to a tea set.
For Carol, for

closed door Ford.
In the meantime
on such a very. Brought

of the current
by no means
which were fabrics

of other uses
yet walled water, yet
lip-synched, the Holy

Ghost catches you
and you fall down.

Fugue

Simultaneous Netherlands
and the simultaneous flowers

sometimes an offal. Tours
in and around the metal bar

preventing fall; last bucket
containing two days wrecks in

from the air. Simultaneous hilts
naming barns. In snow again

separately, volume of accounted-
for shells found around a mountain

extending reeds extending in theme
measure of the world gone hiding

in a "vice grip," as flowers
under cover of thread

simultaneous standing with flu
upon other flu

"into her arms," in a filmed image
major and the minor chords

simultaneous dials for one effect.
Fugue wherein two wives

having the grouse feather, having
the single pearl

lines by a burning down
roof's span. Choke of a peach pit

hinge to hang off from, simultaneous
braille broke in afternoon.

"The whole cast of them in hands passing..."

The whole cast of them in hands passing
Jack's gapped amassed adventure version
reads like Minneapolis at least. And

autograph

my hands with a saying for 10 minutes, specific

as in parking lots in
worse for wear, where for being
sixteen, as age. With

rock salt
in route to
gastanks

if dreamed shouldn't so
much tear away from itself

he said—Christ, its gradual the

rope burn the

finish the

tropes try to talk, either you're
heroic; either you're the children
or you're the grownups.

The clearings, they and him and there
should aside
from so far anyway
saying

they're misfits, all of them
punchdrunk
saying they're

naming names

about Paul Robeson.

very early in the life of jerome (vii)

I am convinced we are surrounded. By pilots, my love, that recommend the way to escape before they start chasing. That greet us with blows once they are over the doorstep. We were not properly introduced and you may come with me if you wish. Much has been made of the resemblance. And the beer run, with Tony, if you are so inclined.

the cartography

On sound of fans, as a figurative
having mistaken

the crows starting
against leaves and

straightened into a basket, under cymbals

for dunes we had returned
with the child's ashes, for the drying

of the surface
on the man made lakes

instead the man made lakes

in a glass
bottomed boat towing a stretcher
from the dock

onto our lawn, in trenches
in order, under balloons

in these bright lamps
tile arrives in baskets and bells

arrive in baskets full of stops
carried on hangers
covering brooch.
Blouses and

blouses and
sand kept pressed
to the uniform.

for japan paper

How that the edge collected only debris, entire fumble of spire for
look of Japan Paper; sea and floor impaling. He had

a scene for forty pictures scene for red hair and lace scene for Paul
Lee and sea founded round; borders pushed badly into her hair.
Japan paper appeared into orange, in explaining a wall, also Japan

burns, made of paper called someday ice edging into a furnace,
called by name and then Paul Lee and hedges so lace so to ravel the
horse's designs into a sea straight down deep into a sea and round.

hammershoi sequence

1.
At the farm building, turned and
in view of a waiting gale, I heard
last strains from the music room, some
hours back, also called resting
young lady and her back to me
under cabinet sofa as resigned, interior

2.
once the young oak trees
and young oak trees in middle
of the rooms, as a
courtyard inside
in all directions, for another of
a brooding group's portrait
in a posture
of the willing.

3.
As surfaced at all, servicing
of the Boston patricians, those closest
to more familiar narrative
members of a private club turned
at waiting gale, in competition.

4.
Like Hopper's figure, life-size sitter
of the flat earth parallel
the kind of fiction in which
the chorus called her Three Graces
Hopper's nude antique, equestrian
figure we never saw.

rehearsals for britain

I have in mind the arch tome, I have
the funnel aimed to sweep in flecks
of paint like those, fallen

upon inspection, face revealing verdict
by viola's tune, by the cello tune
closing to applause, to go on for

other schillings, to save a life and
stand the hands as on a myth with
the hand grenade, with the statuette

from Cuneiform he seemed
to have been reading. Through sand
to course and sand to shake

by right I have the wronged, I have
the beach emptied in a drill in
case of their assault.

canto de ossanha

In ritual sense, in
every age the commemorative heart
as

annotated by absence
as described
in vegetation
through which
procession taking aim
had last lined up
in a parallel
squared off
before them, baring
the holder for
the other holder of plants
as spectrum duplicating
here throughout
the pleasure of the trough
in its relation
to other troughs
instead of writing next time
phone every question
you have about glass
and show of dress and
show of hands
there is
at night
from the comfort of home
for seven months

out of the year
towels that must be left under the door
any number of colors, described
by your wife and nephew
whom I have wanted
to fuck up the ass

in the least of my desires
in ascending order
with their hands
in mine
on the bank of a river.

"You just have to go down a flight of stairs..."

You just have to go down a flight of stairs
and go down a flight of stairs. You
have to bear and
hear the shift in front of cars

or you just topple over into the bath
and topple over into the bath. And
string lights
around the house and
aim blanks at the garage door.
You only have to

find yourself about to slake rust
from around your limbs
and you only have to find yourself
about to slake rust
from around your limbs

and you just have to
find verse to course
through the wood floors
and find verse to course
through the wood floors and

you have to knock
water into your lap and
then fall asleep

and you have
to bundle intrusion

up inside you
and you have to chew on your sleep
as on your husband. And
you have to wait by a dock and
hook sand from out of the bottom

you have to hook sand from out of the bottom
and you only have to
color your lips with music
and loads plums into the icebox.

And you have to load your arm into a sling
and edge your trust into the yellow

and you have to scour your face
and you only have to scour your face. You have to
break vases open over the stones
to find dew inside and
you have to let drool swell up inside you

and let drool swell up inside you
and you have to brush up against ceilings.
And brush up against ceilings and
you just have to string dark
along the frames of doors.

very early in the life of jerome (viii)

Please start with a cover of blanket and please say you will
not leave me until all but one of the guests is gone. When we are
alone with him, he has his keys but I have removed his car from the
drive and planned it at another drive, with a note on the windshield
for Flora, Fauna, and their brother Jim. When I am fourteen on the
diving board, please start by saying I am fifteen and deny you were
ever there. In the township concession stand, gift shop, arboretum,
please fulfill the whims of my commissary with three dollars for
the chips and a dollar for the wax museum. Should I return, please
relieve me of my duties with the pistol, stamen, collection plate;
spread of rumor in a booth as an attempt at telephone, ignoring the
toll; furthermore: the hymen and chest containing instructions to be
amplified up and down the street. No overcoats. No neighbor crying
foul when it is you who should be looking.

plaster of paris

About the product
we are encouraged
to cry out to it on
the bedside table, to verse
all complaints toward
the home office
in Maryland
there are groupings of boys
refusing the toll to pass
among the ends about
the Chesapeake Bay Bridge
we are told please find
enclosed a model
in a plaster of Paris cast
signed by Hilda this
and this year only

the child receives
a discount, pays less for
his trouble, next year
there will be guards
a debtors prison
for any who
cannot not afford to enter.

<u>this is not mythology</u>

not punctual delivery
gravestone marking the site

moreover, no one
to witness symbol
of tap water bound
in a symbol for air

I will never
say I did not
tell you that
after concussion
this is not

a god in front
of the hamper
berating dusk

no banishment
to desert
when it is just

money he is missing. There are

no decent bathrooms and
I have to bunk
under a girl

who pees the bed and
always has denied it
my brother Stephen

is not here
nor our cousin
who kicked him in the balls

the food is terrible
and I won at the dozens

and I fell off a trampoline.

at least the muses

For as long
as I have known them

for participating

I am given

all the toddlers
lost in caves

all the queens
in the castle

so long as

their shoes are fumbled

they will want one of their own

if they don't

I'll see you Wednesday
by the time he reaches Texas

we will already

will have left
with my mother

my confederate; the chorus is

the world is rotten
there is a table

for film advancing
on the wall

of all of them
walking in circles

in the building
is constructed

persons fleeing
a cafeteria

on forest floor

a known guitarist

as we will hear prepared

solution
repeating the formula, varying

combustible
reproductions of graves

assembly on the concourse

pitiful host and hostess

managing coats

as you carry out

a reenactment
of the inhabitant
engaged in

the hall of a terminal

in his position
as a foil

to investment
in continuous topless dancing

in the arms of his daughter

all he has to do

is initiate a blindfold
and have

Mr. Widmark can have
his goddamned

hotline for the funeral home

and have the hotline for the funeral home
is 1-800-DIGNITY. Our very flight
in a likeness of an hour
aside the patient, where there is

no way to show paved ground
from peasant clearing, the only

instance of the grandfather is given
in the highlight film, so

busy he was with the convention, 1986

the last of my tithes was paid
at a service led

by one hundred women in gold hats

there's always one asshole ahead
the road, with a distress signal

flagging his pants. In a diversion

in some such row of Georgia
beside the marble harvest in Jasper; it is

closed and that is why

there are ribbons everywhere
directing whether or not with
proper care to find an entrance

as this on any Saturday, no one
knows anything

about that kind of dementia, of

radio's imploring descent, what

good is hung up
in the wealth to be said

and wealth to be made

from views in parked cars.

Some of my best friends

pretending lamps
for the form's exterior

many the evening hours

touching my hair, someone telling
something as the rerun

of that variety, whose host in isolation

has come elated in a speech
bearing the custom made

blouse instructs, featured in
the final issue of "Two Sermons," at

a lecture in Lime Street, reporting

from a scene, what's to say beyond forgetting

what was known throughout the world
upon arrival

with pails, some of the firemen, so
the great Belizean novel begins

on another continent, with
a chase scene; at least

the muses fleeing a salt spill
continued practice their attempt

at having written
suggestions for departure

from the company, in the lyric
impulse preceding fever

Please believe me when I say

there is more to be done than that
which has already

ended in exclamation with always
bright become shorter, with

the oldest work having been assigned

to the youngest among them to
those as such acquainted

with the hyphenated name

for orange I have invented
and tried to make catch on.

Since being told there was

no other way to wear it
if Perestroika
was already taken
and in its place performed the ballad

"Why couldn't you at least

have closed the door

feigning sleep?" Much as
the face related

in a diagram of a hand-turned clock

the wearer of a gold chain
and glass jaw with night immediately

indicating a wheel tangled in with sticks

adjacent to

an abandoned lot, a chimney
at its center and a hillock

at its center
on earth

as it is

in a Las Vegas–style
floor show, as it is

ground to

an anatomy

as the appropriate forum in which
to have an accident, in time

a sense one has made of her drawings

over top of them and

over top of them, there is

but little satisfaction
in posing nude in front a crucible

tied by one hand

and in the other motioning
land to adjoining craters

for the way of salt

there is a window
out of which can only

come shotgun in the face

in his attempting, lighted

on a cake

swimming to where
we say a truce

in one ear and out of

the same ear

I've only arrival
leading belief
into the distance

in proper burial among
those that refused

the hand provided

with the will
that has the lake

vivid on entrance, while still

while you are under
paused at giving signs

directed nowhere, in obedience

we have moved
the family claim

out of a pasture
to lengthening strange

all letters and cloths
as addressed

care of the sailor
making an icebox
as we have read into her face

the limbs of the dead in a circle

with jewelry

in a fire surrounding the body

as several manner
of glossy phonograph recordings

when he is ten

of the former Dolores Hamilton
married ambassador heard

in the background

proclaiming virtue in the sink

as mother has described
for a willing audience

each of his birthdays
in oak editions, eighteen

grafts of the skin, included in Atlantic Records'

limited edition

box set of knives
of killers caught on tape

in company of orchard
a flock assembled

to take me out of my house

where I am given
cuts in my hands

so that the skin should break open
having attended
a style of house described

in the form of a question

on the condition, on
a see-saw regarding

the right of old

to slight adventure

in a distance of tunnel

on an empty stomach, with

a manual for
assembling walls to

keep out water

when in years past
they made their way

with the film
I have of sleep

in worshipful balance

in domesticating

a neighboring island

as belated
to be sure he is not collared

in an armed robbery

believe you are speaking
throughout the residence

of pressure on your throat

as the barrack landmarked
and the garage's landmark

all property as it is forwarded

to a spinster, if she was
not deserving already

here is further proof

I became short of breath describing
the burglar's own plans to him

along a horizon

you will find maps

for where you are standing

before you are turned
into the shape
and centered below his seat
as extended

into weather.
We have to describe
the flag football game
to blind people and

fill out a questionnaire

as to which dress you would choose

such is the novelty
among difference

you can say

an aphorism, a resemblance
to the outside; world

given number

and place displayed

I couldn't admire him
any less for his courage

in the line of duty
specific temperatures

have vanished

and our kayak
has vanished and

we will not allow

any to be ushered
into a four o'clock showing

of lantern slides

containing the motto
for bottom

stored for safekeeping
in a dialect.
Neither the opposite

kind in fainting

upon command. Our basis
for our opinion

on the first dozen
rudimentary expeditions
on private property

the raft anticipates

its position

in an emergency

the chaplain knows

when he is needed on horseback when
he will announce that

to be heard

over narration
and entrance

into the column

the engineering

has a duration
and a recurring character

repeatedly discarding
a racing form
committing
the measurement

of outburst
to his memory

barred from the fashionable term
of a year abroad

at the hostage broadcast
and prayer breakfast

the lap dance
is a tribute

to abominable meadow

I will write later in life

suitably placed
in an outdoor and

floral model
of earlier rooms.

notes:

The title "Prayer" is borrowed from a Beach Boys song. It also contains a line from the Billy Joel song "Uptown Girl."

"... my little big mouth bass ..." in "Very Early in the Life of Jerome (i)" is quoted from Eric Sosnoff.

"19 Names for our band" contains banter by Dear Nora, Kate Schapira, and Barbara Edwards.

"When delivering make-up" is for Kate Schatz and contains a headline from the cover of *Ebony,* December 2004 issue.

"Like Molly in The Mountain Lion" contains parts of various lines from J.M. Coetzee's *Stranger Shores: Literary Essays: 1986-1999* and Joyce Carol Oates' *Them.*

"Notes on Camp" is for Laida Lertxundi. Its title is borrowed from a Susan Sontag essay.

"... going bazookas ..." in "The Blowjob Pictures" is quoted from *Vice* Magazine's "DOs and DONTs"

"Sonnet (In this country you have ...)" contains parts of an interview with Jhumpa Lahiri in the *New York Times Magazine,* September 7, 2003.

The title "Where Are the Negroes in Hartford, Connecticut?" is borrowed from a collage by Xaiviera Simmons.

"Dan Eldon's sister Amy/more rockabilly singers" in "Poem Beginning With a Line from Edward McKeever" is (obviously) quoted from Edward McKeever. For the use of this line (I suppose) I am also indebted to Robert Duncan's "A Poem Beginning with a Line by Pindar."

The title "Juliet of the Spirits" is borrowed from a Federico Fellini film.

"Palimpsest" contains parts of various lines from Ann Cummins' "Red Ant House."

The title "Cantos de Ossanha" is borrowed from a Baden Powell song.

"This is not Mythology" is for Erica Saleh to make up for being an asshole.

acknowledgements:

"For Japan Paper" and "You would suppose that. In solving the way." originally appeared in *3rd Bed*.

"Very Early in the Life of Jerome (i, ii, iii, iv, v, and vi)" in *6x6*.

"Poem" in *Aufgabe*.

"Funeral, Mineral, Vegetable," "Prayer," and "Fugue" in *Bat City Review*.

"If we believe theory," "In An Uncurling Game," "Those turned quiet by knives, by night...," "Very Early in the Life of Jerome (vii)," and "You just have to go down a flight of stairs..." in *The Bedazzler*.

"Anyone can purchase flags...," "Sonnet (In this country you have...)," "Oftener, golden rule; nude...," "Palimpsest," and "Diamond Zones" in *Boston Review*.

"Where Are the Negroes in Hartford, Connecticut?," "When delivering make-up...," and "The Blowjob Pictures" in *Court Green*.

"Sonnet (So long does reason go...)" in *Clerestory*.

"Framework," "In An Uncurling Game," "And what is more but the glare of dust...," "Juliet of the Spirits," "For Indian Hidden," "This is not mythology," and "The Whole cast of them in hands passing..." in *Fence*.

"Wilderness Literature" in *FO A RM*.

"Sonnet (So long does reason go…)," "Rehearsals for Britain,"
"Abigail," "On Television," and "Four inter-titles for our music
video" (as "One Governs Oneself") in the *Grolier Poetry Prize
Annual,* 2004.

"You just have to go down a flight of stairs…" in *New Orleans
Review.*

Thanks to: My family, of course, and Dawn Michelle Baude, Anna
Bohichik, Tisa Bryant, Mary Caponegro, Tyler Carter, Robert Creeley
(r.i.p.), Thalia Field, Erika Howsare, Caroline Knox, Ann Lauterbach,
Christian Nagler, Michael Nicoloff, Seth Perlow, Joan Retallack, Kate
Schapira, Kate Schatz, Leonard Schwartz, Lori Shine, Stephen Shore,
Xaviera Simmons, Eric Sosnoff, Christopher Stackhouse, Kate Wolf,
Rebecca Wolff, Keith Waldrop, Diane Williams, and C.D. Wright

Fence Books is an extension of *Fence,* a biannual journal of poetry, fiction, art, and criticism that has a mission to redefine the terms of accessibility by publishing challenging writing distinguished by idiosyncrasy and intelligence rather than by allegiance with camps, schools, or cliques. It is part of our press's mission to support writers who might otherwise have difficulty being recognized because their work doesn't answer to either the mainstream or to recognizable modes of experimentation.

The Motherwell Prize (formerly the Alberta Prize) is an annual series that offers publication of a first or second book of poems by a woman, as well as a one thousand dollar cash prize.

Our second prize series is the Fence Modern Poets Series. This contest is open to poets of any gender and at any stage of career, and offers a one thousand dollar cash prize in addition to book publication.

For more information about either prize, visit www.fencebooks.com, or send an SASE to: Fence Books/[Name of Prize], New Library 320, University at Albany, 1400 Washington Avenue, Albany, NY, 12222.

For more about *Fence,* visit www.fenceportal.org.

fence books

THE MOTHERWELL PRIZE

Unspoiled Air	Kaisa Ullsvik Miller

THE ALBERTA PRIZE

The Cow	Ariana Reines
Practice, Restraint	Laura Sims
A Magic Book	Sasha Steensen
Sky Girl	Rosemary Griggs
The Real Moon of Poetry and Other Poems	Tina Brown Celona
Zirconia	Chelsey Minnis

FENCE MODERN POETS SERIES

Star in the Eye	James Shea
Structure of the Embryonic Rat Brain	Christopher Janke
The Stupefying Flashbulbs	Daniel Brenner
Povel	Geraldine Kim
The Opening Question	Prageeta Sharma
Apprehend	Elizabeth Robinson
The Red Bird	Joyelle McSweeney

ANTHOLOGIES & CRITICAL WORKS

Not for Mothers Only: Contemporary Poets on Child-Getting & Child-Rearing   Catherine Wagner & Rebecca Wolff, editors

FREE CHOICE POETRY

Rogue Hemlocks	Carl Martin
19 Names for Our Band	Jibade Khalil Huffman
Bad Bad	Chelsey Minnis
Snip Snip!	Tina Brown Celona
Yes, Master	Michael Earl Craig
Swallows	Martin Corless-Smith
Folding Ruler Star	Aaron Kunin
The Commandrine and Other Poems	Joyelle McSweeney
Macular Hole	Catherine Wagner
Nota	Martin Corless-Smith
Father of Noise	Anthony McCann
Can You Relax in My House	Michael Earl Craig
Miss America	Catherine Wagner

FREE CHOICE FICTION

Flet: A Novel	Joyelle McSweeney
The Mandarin	Aaron Kunin